How to Draw
A SAILING CAT

Joy Sikorski

and 99 Other Adventurous Things

STERLING

New York / London

To Emily, Michael, and Dimas

STERLING and the distinctive Sterling logo are registered trademarks of Sterling Publishing Co., Inc.

10 9 8 7 6 5 4 3 2 1

Published by Sterling Publishing Co., Inc.
387 Park Avenue South, New York, NY 10016
Text and Illustrations © 2009 by Joy Sikorski
Distributed in Canada by Sterling Publishing
c/o Canadian Manda Group, 165 Dufferin Street, Toronto, Ontario, Canada M6K 3H6
Distributed in the United Kingdom by GMC Distribution Services, Castle Place,
166 High Street, Lewes, East Sussex, England BN7 1XU
Distributed in Australia by Capricorn Link (Australia) Pty. Ltd.,
PO Box 704, Windsor, NSW 2756, Australia

Sterling ISBN 978-1-4027-5707-5

The artwork for this book was created using pencil, watercolor, acrylic, and a Mac.

For information about custom editions, special sales, premium and corporate purchases,
please contact Sterling Special Sales Department at 800-805-5489 or
specialsales@sterlingpublishing.com.

Introduction

Dear Reader,

Drawing is easy and fun! I'll shout it from the rooftops!

That's why I wrote this book. Little Man is the main character—he's my cat who always comes back. He's an outside cat. When Little Man comes back with muddy paws and a leaf stuck to his tail, you wonder just where he has been and what went on. In *How to Draw a Sailing Cat*, we find out what Little Man has been up to in the marsh lands near his house. We also learn to draw 99 interesting and adventurous things, among which are a fox, a tugboat, and a goat eating a tin can. Get out your colors and some paper!

Oh, and remember: It's OK to smudge.

Love,
Joy

Lesson 1
Little Man the Cat

Tip: His ears are an "M" shape.

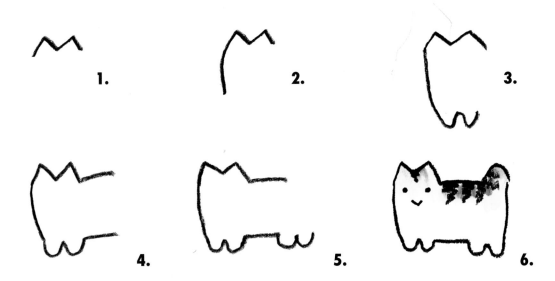

1.

2.

3.

4.

5.

6.

Tip: Practice placement of eyes and nose to get the perfect expression. If you make his nose too pointy he'll look like an owl.

"Mew!" "Mew!" "Who!"

Lesson 2
The House Where Little Man Lives

Tip: Start with an "L" shape.

Lesson 3
Clouds

Tip: Start with a "3" shape. Leave spaces between your lines, and your cloud will look fluffy.

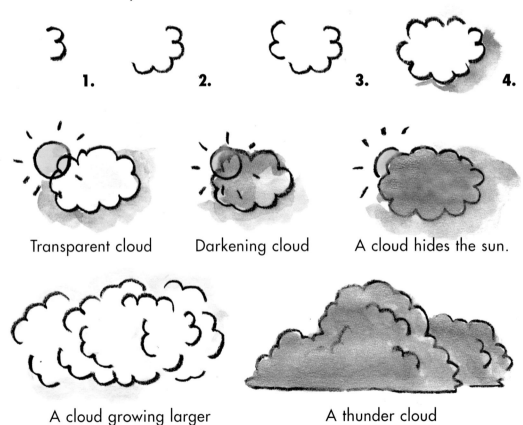

1. 2. 3. 4.

Transparent cloud   Darkening cloud   A cloud hides the sun.

A cloud growing larger   A thunder cloud

Lesson 4
Lightning!

Tip: Start with a "7" shape for lightning. Make your lightning flashes illuminate your dark clouds!

1.

2.

3.

Tip: To make Little Man look up, tilt his ears back and make his eyes and nose high on his face.

Lesson 5
Window with Curtains

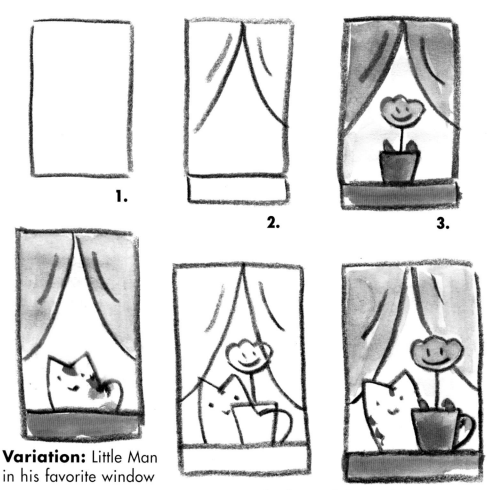

1.

2.

3.

Variation: Little Man
in his favorite window

Tip: Erase the lines of things that are behind.

Tip: Grass is a lot like rain, except that it's all in a row.

Big raindrops fall and Little Man runs home.

Lesson 6
Flower in a Pot

Flowers are happy little souls.

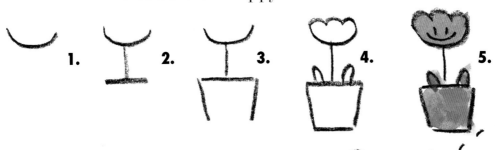

1. 2. 3. 4. 5.

Bonus: How to draw a falling flower pot

Variations: a sunflower, a tulip, and a fancy drinking glass (Follow steps 1 and 2 first.)

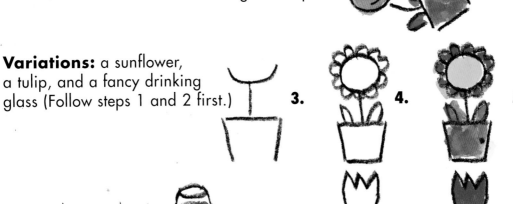

3. 4. 5.

1. 2. 3. 4. 5.

Tip: Draw rows of wavy lines to show rising water.

Weather report: Heavy rains and high winds today! Little Man accidentally bumps the flower pot off the window sill, sending the flower on an adventure!

11

Lesson 7
Splashes: How to Make Water Look Wet

1. 2. 3.

1. 2. 3. 4.

Tip: Tilt his ears forward and angle his eyes and nose to make Little Man look down.

Bonus: Fishie 1.   2.   3.   4.

Little Man watches as the puddle grows deeper.   13

Lesson 8
Leaves, Ants, and Bugs

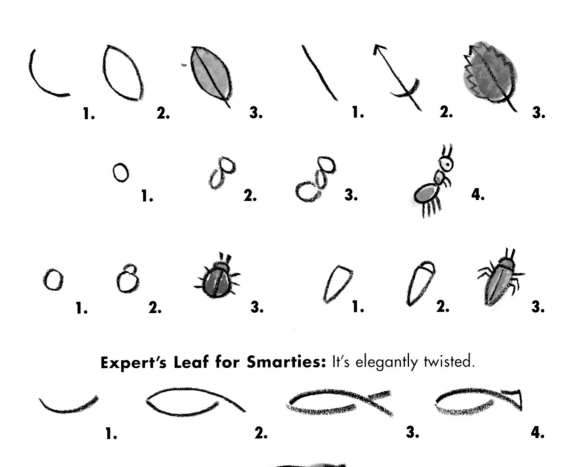

Expert's Leaf for Smarties: It's elegantly twisted.

A puddle is an ocean if you're an ant.

Oh my gosh! The flower pot is completely underwater!

15

Lesson 9
A "Killie"

Did you know?
"Kill" is a very old word. It means "stream." A Killie lives in a kill.

 **1.**

 **2.**

 **3.**

 **4.**

 **5.**

 **6.**

 **7.**

 **8.**

 **9.**

Lesson 10
Fish Splash

1. **2.** **3.**

Tip: If you know how to draw the expert's leaf on page 14, you can also make a leaping fish!

Lesson 11
Open Door

Tip: To be sure your open door lines up nicely with the door frame, imagine that you can see the whole door frame with x-ray eyes.

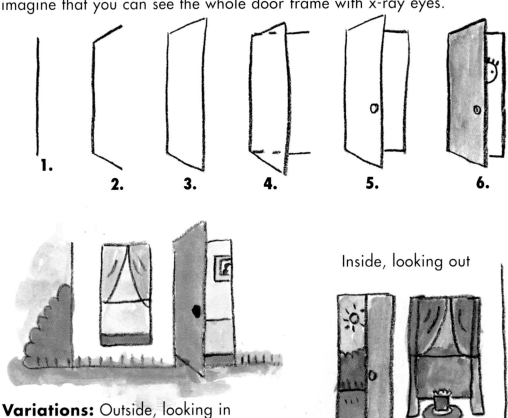

Variations: Outside, looking in

Inside, looking out

The rain stops, the wind goes away, and the sun comes out.
Little Man jumps from his doorstep to go on an adventure.

Lesson 12
Little Man Running

1.

2.

3.

4.

5.

Note all-important hop marks.

6.

Lesson 13
Reflection

Little Man pauses to admire his ripply reflection in a puddle.

Tip: For a reflection, turn your drawing upside down and draw with squiggly lines.

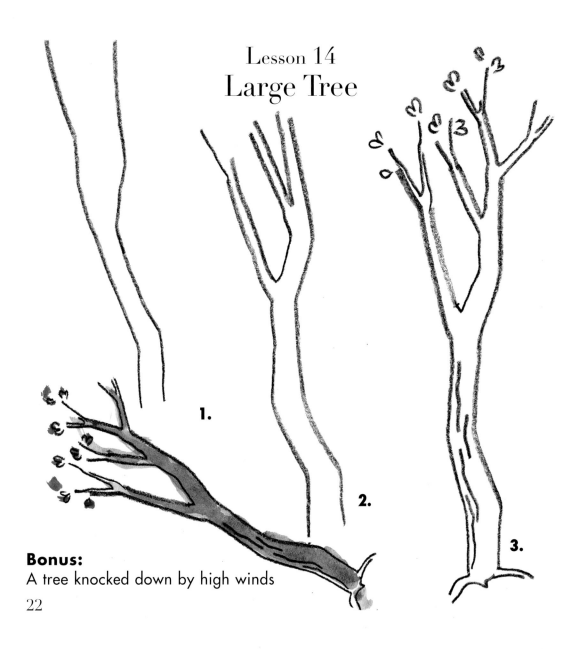

Large Tree

1.

2.

3.

Bonus:
A tree knocked down by high winds

Little Man crosses the brook on the fallen tree and scampers into the marshes where he has never been before!

Lesson 15
Marsh Plants

Cattail

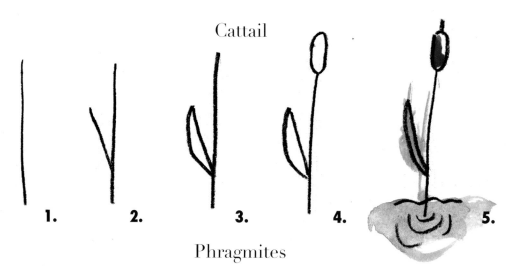

1.   2.   3.   4.   5.

Phragmites

Be a pro: Say "Frag-MY-teez." It's Latin for reeds, you know.

1.   2.   3.   4.   5.

Lesson 16
Ducklings in a Row

1.   **2.**   **3.**   **4.**   25

Lesson 17
Ducklings' First Swim

1. 2. 3. 4. 5.

6. 7. 8. 9.

Tip: I always leave spaces between my lines, and then I connect them, if I feel like it.

Lesson 18
Make Way for Ducklings!

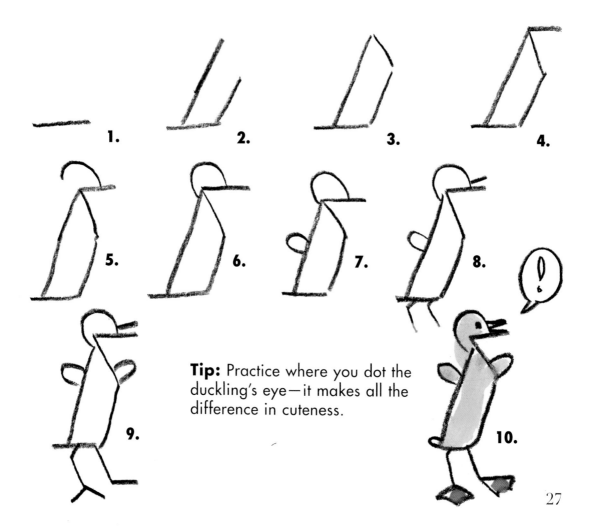

1.

2.

3.

4.

5.

6.

7.

8.

9.

Tip: Practice where you dot the duckling's eye—it makes all the difference in cuteness.

10.

Lesson 19
Field of Phragmites

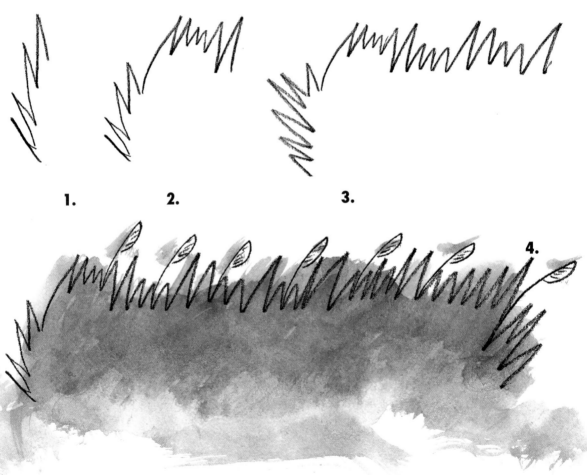

1.

2.

3.

4.

Lesson 20
Redwing Blackbird

"O-ka-REEEEEE !"

1.   2.   3.   4.   5.

Lesson 21
High Tide

Lesson 22
Low Tide

With bonus crab
and snail lessons

31

Lesson 23
Dragonfly

1. **2.** **3.** **4.** **5.**

6.

Bonus: How to draw Little Man's paw, which he lifts up in a tentative way when wondering.

1. **2.** **3.**

Lesson 24
Bullfrog

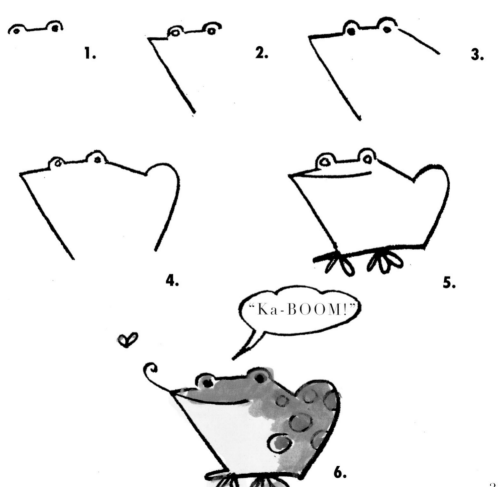

1.

2.

3.

4.

5.

"Ka-BOOM!"

6.

Ducks: Mallard and Bufflehead

The marsh is filled with all kinds of birds of different colors. Little Man is fascinated.

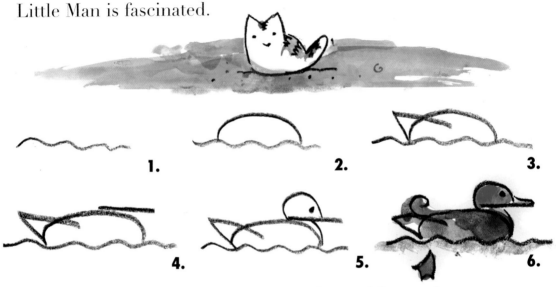

1. 2. 3.

4. 5. 6.

Note the Mallard's orange webbed feet paddling in the water.

"Bufflehead" means "large head," but it also can mean silly or foolish.

1. 2. 3.

Know the Ducks

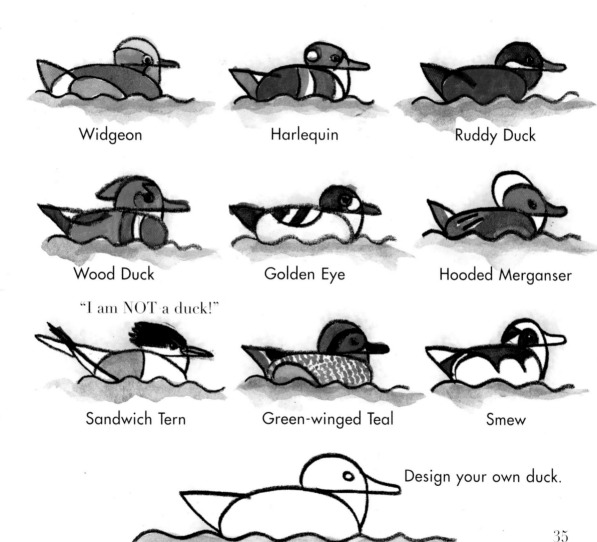

Widgeon

Harlequin

Ruddy Duck

Wood Duck

Golden Eye

Hooded Merganser

"I am NOT a duck!"

Sandwich Tern

Green-winged Teal

Smew

Design your own duck.

Lesson 26
Canada Goose

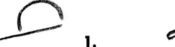 **1.**

 2.

 3.

Tip: Start with a baseball hat shape.

4.

5.

6.

7.

8.

Lesson 27
Geese Migrating North

1.

2.

3.

"Honk! Honk!"

4.

Expert's Geese for Smarties:
How to draw them flapping their
wings up and down.

3.

"Wonk! Wonk!"

2.

1.

W N S E

"Kreekity-kweek!"

37

Lesson 28
Fox

1.

2.

3.

4.

5.

6.

7.

Animal babies:
 Fox kits have small bodies and big heads, which makes them extra cute.

Lesson 29
Yellow Swallowtail Butterfly

1.   **2.**   **3.**   **4.**   **5.**

Expert's Advice for Smarties: It looks hard, but if you follow along you can make a very nice one on the first try.

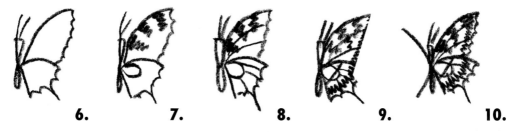

6.   **7.**   **8.**   **9.**   **10.**

Draw the butterfly's other wing.

11.

Variation:
Try drawing one wing flattened to make your butterfly flutter.

Flight paths are loopy fun.

Fox Side View

1.

2.

3.

Both the fox and Little Man followed the beautiful butterfly, enchanted. They were quite surprised to meet one another!

"Eek!"

"Eek!"

"Eek!"

41

Lesson 31
Northern Diamondback Terrapin

Otherwise known as a turtle!

1. **2.** **3.**

4. **5.**

6. **7.**

Tip: Their eyes are high on their heads, so they can see above water.

8.

Lesson 32
Muskrat

1.

2.

3.

4.

5.

6.

7.

1.

2.

Muskrat swimming

3.

Note: Their lodge is called a "pushup."

Lesson 33
Toy Sail Boat

1.

2.

3.

4.

5.

A fun activity:
Say "toy boat" fast 10 times.

POLKA DOT

6.

44

Little Man finds a comfortable little toy sail boat and jumps into it, perhaps to have a catnap.

Lesson 34
Little Man in a Toy Sail Boat

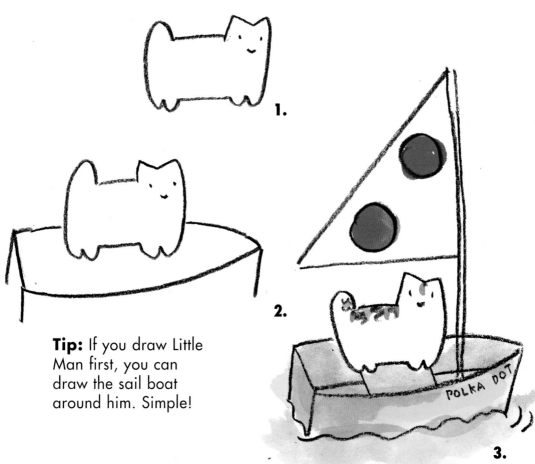

1.

2.

Tip: If you draw Little Man first, you can draw the sail boat around him. Simple!

POLKA DOT

3.

Lesson 35
Catnaps

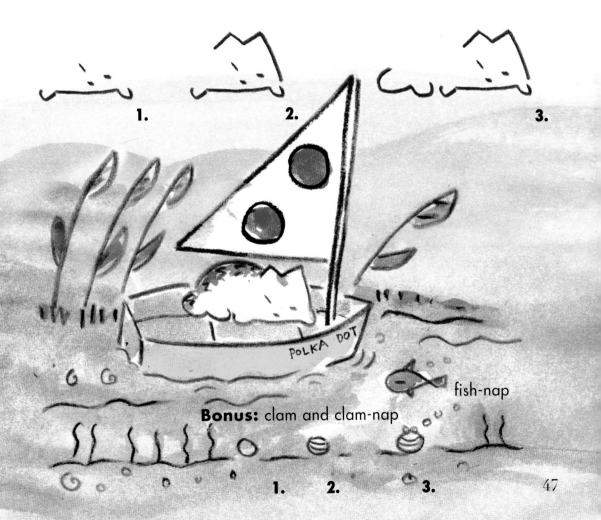

1. 2. 3.

POLKA DOT

fish-nap

Bonus: clam and clam-nap

1. 2. 3.

Lesson 36
Little Man Dreams of Dots

1.

2.

3.

4.

POLKA DOT

Lesson 37
The Dream in the *Polka Dot* Boat

A splash awakens Little Man from his nap. His sailboat, the *Polka Dot*, is drifting out to sea with the tide.

As Little Man sails away, his house, the fallen tree, and the fox look very small in the distance.

Advice: You don't have to catch fish, just attract their attention.

Lesson 38
Squid

POLKA DOT

1.

2.

3.

4.

5.

6.

52

Draw Little Man very large and he will look close to you.

Bonus: Flying fish

1.

2.

Note flotsam and jetsam, otherwise known as junk!

POLKA DOT

"Junk? Not me!"

Lesson 39
Dolphin

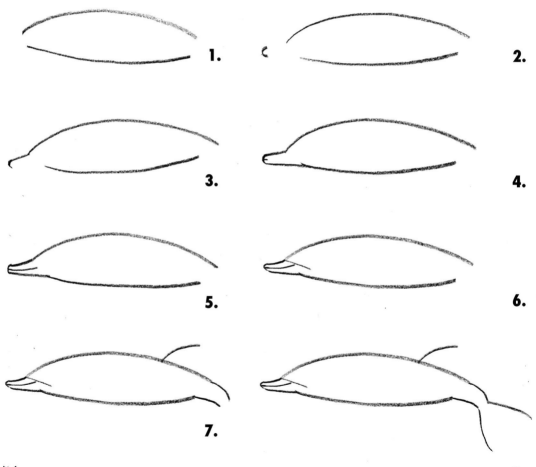

1.

2.

3.

4.

5.

6.

7.

8.

A big dolphin accompanies Little Man on his voyage.

9.

10.

Variation: Talking dolphin

1.   2.   3.   4.

5.

"Crick! Eh-eh-eh!"

Lesson 40
Coral Reef

Little Man looks down into the water and sees many wonderful things.

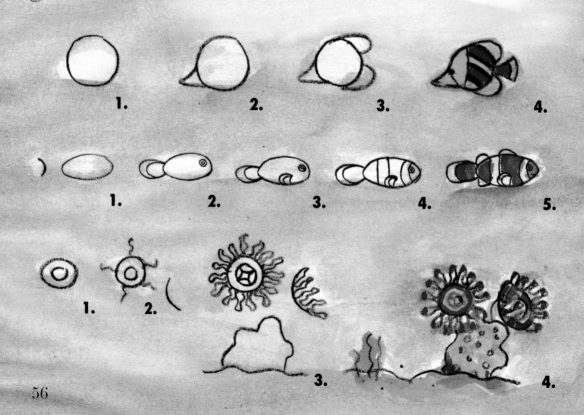

1.   2.   3.   4.

1.   2.   3.   4.   5.

1.   2.   3.   4.

Lesson 41
Reef Fish

57

Lesson 42
Octopus

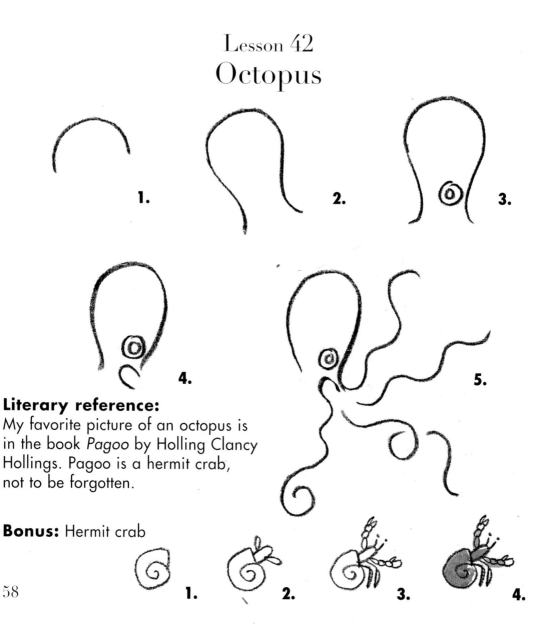

1.

2.

3.

4.

5.

Literary reference:
My favorite picture of an octopus is
in the book *Pagoo* by Holling Clancy
Hollings. Pagoo is a hermit crab,
not to be forgotten.

Bonus: Hermit crab

1.

2.

3.

4.

58

Finishing touches:
Fatten up the tentacles and add suckers. Then color your octopus in mysterious inky colors.

59

Lesson 43
Buoy Colors

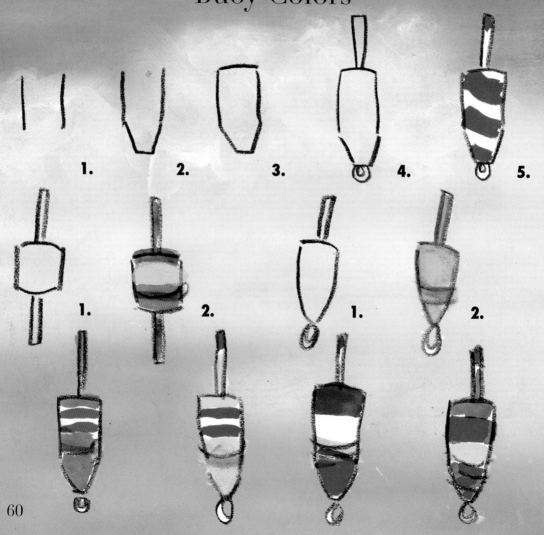

1.　　　2.　　　3.　　　4.　　　5.

1.　　　2.　　　1.　　　2.

60

Sky Colors

Little Man sees something in the distance. An island? Or is it only clouds on the horizon?

Lesson 44
Farmhouse

1.

2.

3.

4.

5.

6.

7.

Lesson 45
Barn

1.

2.

3.

As the *Polka Dot* drifts closer, Little Man discovers that the island has a farm on it.

View from the *Polka Dot*

Lesson 46
Kinglet Bird

1.

2.

3.

4.

View from the island

POLKA DOT

Lesson 47
Big Friendly Farm Dog

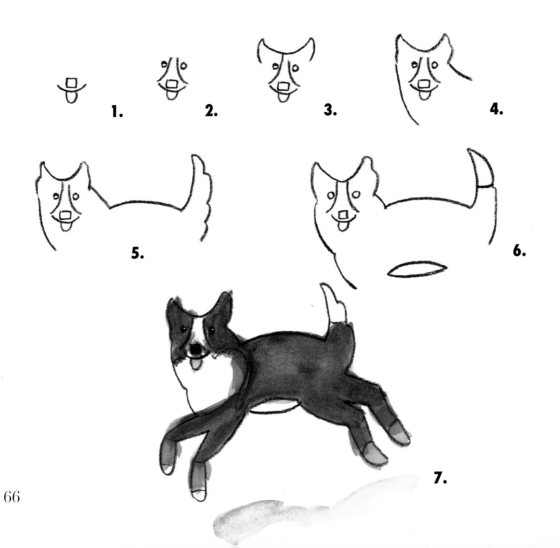

1.

2.

3.

4.

5.

6.

7.

Barn cats watch Little Man
sail past their farm.
A horse eating hay
looks out from the
barn window.

1.

2.

3.

4.

Lesson 48
Horse

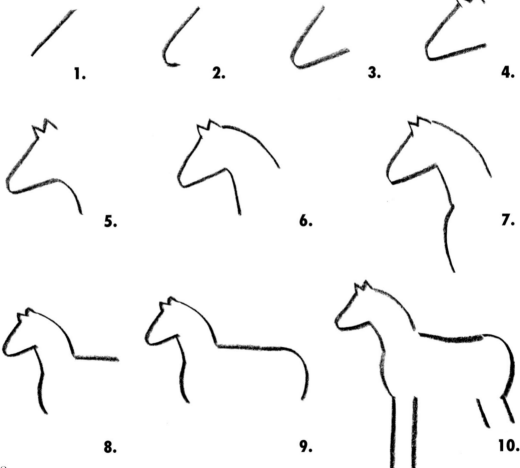

1.

2.

3.

4.

5.

6.

7.

8.

9.

10.

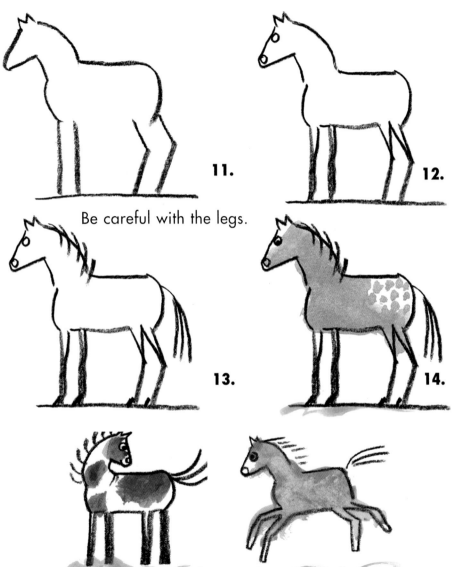

11.

Be careful with the legs.

12.

13.

14.

Note: Don't fret! Simple legs work just as well.

Lesson 49
Cute Baby Pony

1.

2.

3.

4.

5.

6.

7.

8.

9.

Lesson 50
Piglet

Baby pigs are the cutest!

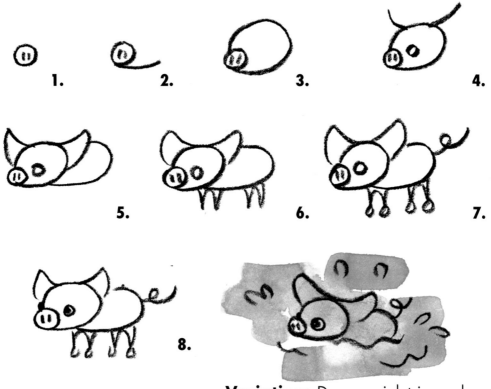

1.
2.
3.
4.
5.
6.
7.
8.

Variation: Draw a piglet in mud.
See Splashes, page 12.

Lesson 51
Hen and Chicks

1. 2. 3.

4. 5. 6.

7. 8. 9.

1. 2. 3. 4.

Lesson 52
Rooster

1.

2.

3.

4.

5.

6.

7.

8.

9.

Lesson 53
Goat

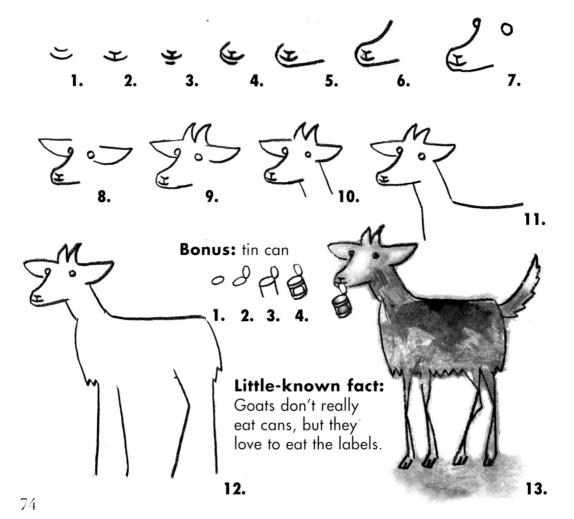

1.   2.   3.   4.   5.   6.   7.

8.   9.   10.   11.

Bonus: tin can

1.   2.   3.   4.

Little-known fact:
Goats don't really
eat cans, but they
love to eat the labels.

12.   13.

POLKA DOT

Lesson 54
Tree

1.

2.

3.

POLKA DOT

Kingfisher

1.   **2.**   **3.**   **4.**   **5.**

Lesson 56
Bear

Tip: The eyes are close together.

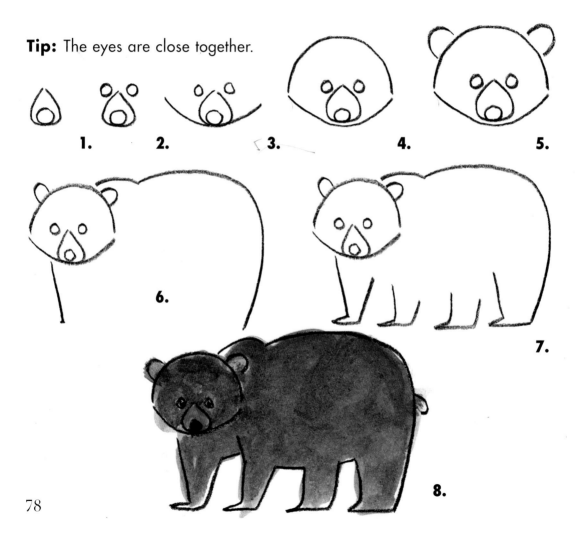

1.

2.

3.

4.

5.

6.

7.

8.

Lesson 57
Bear Cubs

Tip: Place cub's eyes far apart and low, for cuteness.

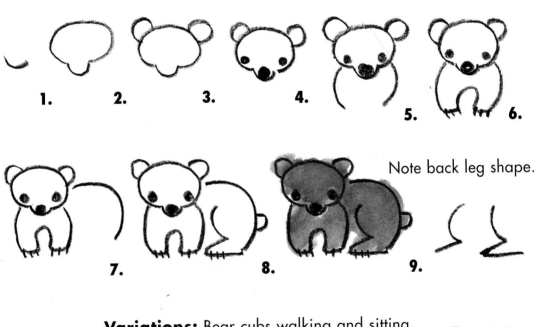

1.   2.   3.   4.   5.   6.

7.   8.   9.

Note back leg shape.

Variations: Bear cubs walking and sitting.

Note back leg shape.

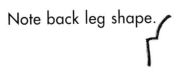

At the edge of the farm, bears are playing in the tree house and picking berries from the bushes.

1.

2.

3.

Bonus: twitter bird

The tide shifts and the *Polka Dot* slowly turns around.
Little Man finds himself heading back along the shore.

POLKA DOT

1. 2. 3. 4. 5. 6.

7. 8. 9. 10.

Bonus: Dog's face in profile. This one is a Bernese mountain dog, for those who like dogs.

As the *Polka Dot* drifts homeward with the incoming tide, Little Man hears a low, deep sound float over the water.

Lesson 58
Tugboat

1.

2.

3.

4.

5.

6.

7.

8.

9.

10.

The *Polka Dot* runs aground in a familiar place, and Little Man hops ashore.

Lesson 59
Feeding a Hungry Baby Bird

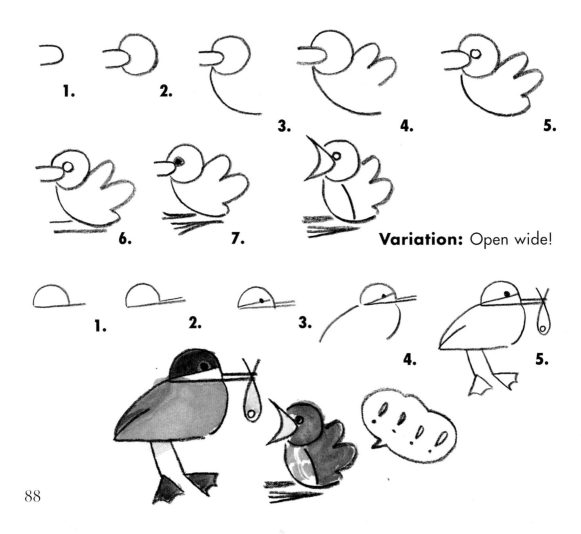

1.

2.

3.

4.

5.

6.

7.

Variation: Open wide!

1.

2.

3.

4.

5.

It's dinnertime in the marsh.

Lesson 60
Weather Vanes and Silhouettes

1.

2. N

3. W N E S

4. W N S E

Note rising tide! Run, Little Man!

"Little Man, where have you been hiding all day?"

Little Man watches the moon rise above the marsh and over the sea. What adventures will nighttime bring?

Map of Where Little Man Lives

Bonus: Lighthouse

1.   2.   3.   4.   5.   6.   7.

Index of Drawing Lessons

1.

2.

3.

4.

Bonus:
swamp rose mallow

Colophon

The tools that I used to make this book

I always have my Prismacolor black pencil number 935 and a sharpener with me. I have a set of watercolors and some brushes. I try lots of different ways to color and I don't mind smudges and drips—they are fun!

I used two typefaces in this book. This typeface is Didot and this typeface is Futura. As for the dots, they come from a pack of dot stickers.

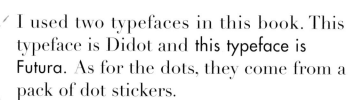

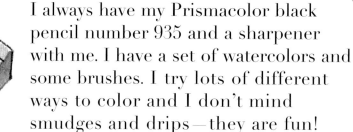